TAILS
OF THE
UNEXPECTED

A JOURNAL OF MEMORIES &
MISADVENTURES FOR MY CAT

Hardie Grant

QUADRILLE

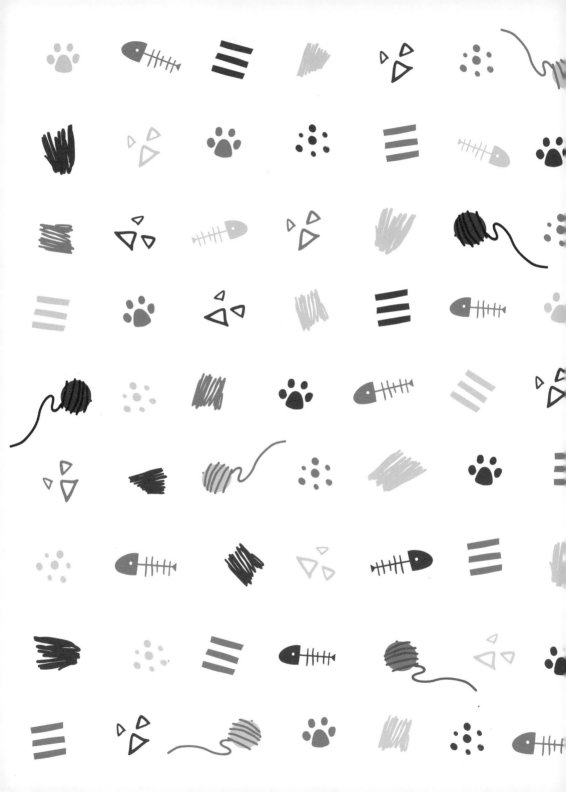

THIS JOURNAL BELONGS TO

_____

FIRST
YEAR

How did you choose your furry friend?

What is their gender?

What did you first notice about them?

What makes them top cat in your eyes?

Did you choose to adopt or buy your furry friend?

Was your cat raised with its mother?

By the end of your first visit was your cat friendly? Nervous? Fearful?

How long did you have to wait between the first visit and taking them home with you?

What were you most excited for with your new four-legged friend?
Cuddles? Playtime?

_____

_____

_____

_____

_____

_____

_____

_____

_____

_____

_____

zzz...

How did you first meet? Was it love at first sight?

_____

_____

_____

_____

_____

_____

_____

_____

_____

_____

_____

_____

_____

_____

As a new owner of a feline, did you have any worries or fears?

How was the journey home with your new cat?

How did you spend your first day together?

Bringing a new family member home for the first time can be a special and un-fur-gettable experience. What are some of your favourite memories from this day?

How did you prepare your home for the new arrival?

Was there any confusion when you first brought your cat home?

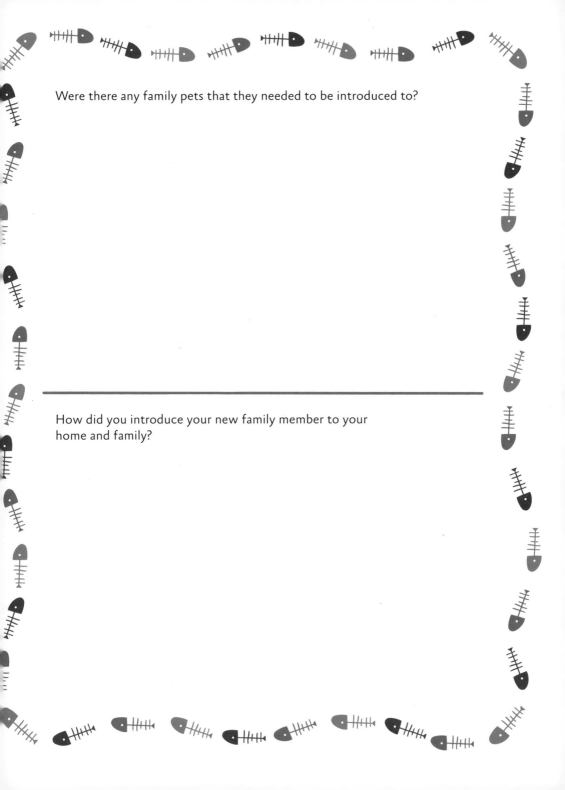

Were there any family pets that they needed to be introduced to?

How did you introduce your new family member to your home and family?

Make a list of all the things you needed to make them feel at home (bed/collar/bowl/toys).

Make a list of anything you still need.

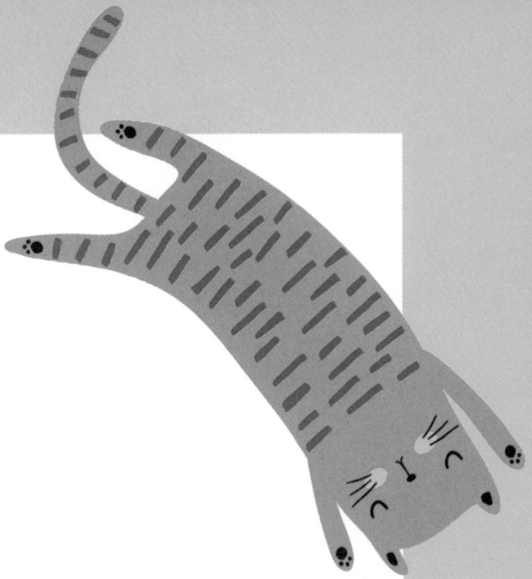

-
-
-
-
-

STICK PHOTOGRAPHS HERE FROM THEIR FIRST YEAR

How and why did you choose your cat's name?

_____

Describe the first time you used their name and they recognised it.

What was their first meal in their new home?

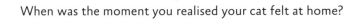

When was the moment you realised your cat felt at home?

How did you celebrate their first birthday?

What was the first gift you got for them?

What was the first gift they brought you?

What happened the first time you went away without your cat?
Describe the experience.

STICK PHOTOGRAPHS HERE FROM ONE YEAR LATER

How does your cat get on with other animals?

Who is your kitty's BFF (best furry friend) and what do they get up to together?

How do they get along with other humans?

_____

_____

_____

_____

_____

_____

_____

_____

_____

_____

_____

_____

_____

_____

_____

DIP YOUR CAT'S PAW IN (NON-TOXIC) PAINT OR INK, THEN GENTLY PRESS IT ONTO THE PAGE FOR A COUPLE OF SECONDS. LIFT THE PAW STRAIGHT UP AND WASH IT.

ROUTINE

How does your cat train you and what is the funniest thing they've done to put you in your place?

What ridiculous things have you tried in the quest for kitty co-operation?

How do you train your cat? What works, what doesn't?

-

-

-

-

-

How well behaved are they?

What's your cat's favourite reward?

Describe your first attempts at toilet training.

Describe your first trip to the vet together.

Is your cat a stay-at-home kitty or a feline explorer?

What happened the first time you let your cat out?

Where's the most surprising place you've found your kitty?

Is your feline part of a catty crew, or do they prefer to run solo?

DRAW OR STICK IN PHOTOGRAPHS OF YOUR CAT'S CREW

Is your cat an early-to-bed kitty or a dirty stop out?

_____

Where's your cat's safe place?

What do you love most about your furry friend?

_____

_____

_____

_____

_____

_____

_____

_____

_____

_____

_____

_____

Whether chomping on cheesy cat biscuits or going gourmet with fresh salmon, food is always the cat's whiskers. What kind of eater is your kitty and what are their top three meal choices?

Do you have any funny food-related stories about your cat?

How has their palate changed as they've got older?

How about human food? What surprising snacks does your cat crave?

List any special dietary requirements.

-
-
-

FAVOURITES

It's definitely called a 'cat nap' for a reason. Where is your cat's preferred snoozing spot?

Where is your preferred spot to snooze together?

What about sleeping positions? Describe or draw their cutest pose.

What is your favourite game to play together?

What is their favourite game to play alone?

A tickle on the tum is a pleasurable experience for giver and receiver; what's your cat's favourite tickle spot?

Every cat has a favourite plaything; what does your cat rate as top toy?

A pampered cat is the cat that got the cream. How does your cat like to be pampered?

Does your furry-legged friend have a favourite hiding place?

List some of the places you have found them hiding.

-
-
-
-
-

What makes your cat purr with passion?

From snooze, stretch, yawn and repeat, what are your cat's favourite activities?

What is their ultimate kitty comfort food?

When it comes to al fresco dining, what does your cat like to catch and eat?

What is your favourite part of the day with your cat and why?

_____

_____

_____

_____

_____

_____

_____

_____

_____

_____

_____

_____

Describe your proudest moment together.

_____

_____

_____

_____

_____

_____

_____

_____

_____

_____

_____

_____

_____

Describe a memorable adventure you've shared together.

_____

_____

_____

_____

_____

_____

_____

_____

_____

_____

_____

_____

Describe a misadventure you've shared together.

_____

_____

_____

_____

_____

_____

_____

_____

_____

_____

_____

Cats are zen and know how to chill out; describe a time when your cat helped you de-stress.

Whether it's the smell of a freshly cooked dinner or a game of 'trip up the owner when they're coming down the stairs', what's the one thing your feline can't resist?

Describe a treasured memory of your cat; this could be an experience you've shared or just a moment in time.

Name the lap of choice for your cat?

_____

Who is your cat's favourite human and how can you tell?

From vacuum cleaners to toilet lids, what household objects strike fear into your otherwise fearless feline?

-
-
-
-
-

STICK PHOTOGRAPHS HERE OF YOUR CAT WITH THEIR
FAVOURITE HUMANS

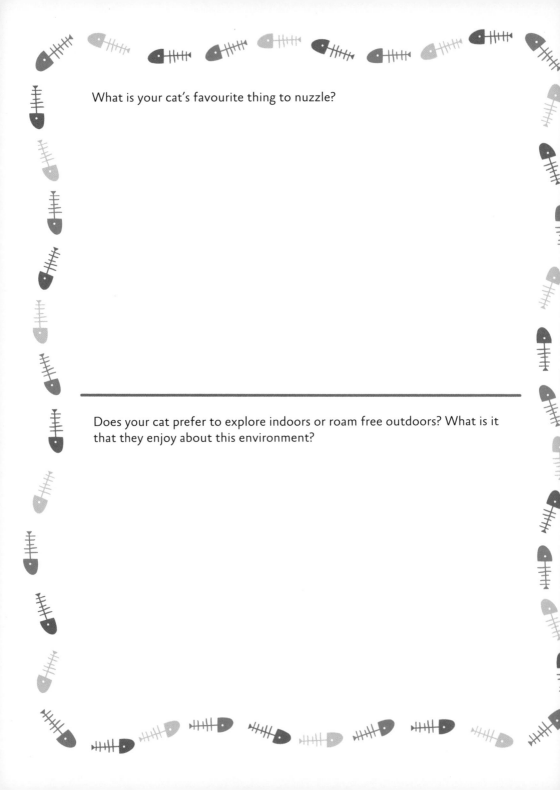

What is your cat's favourite thing to nuzzle?

Does your cat prefer to explore indoors or roam free outdoors? What is it that they enjoy about this environment?

What does your cat do to relax? An early morning scratch session, a long sleep in a cosy corner or an afternoon of bird watching?

_____

_____

_____

_____

_____

_____

_____

_____

_____

_____

_____

DESCRIBE YOUR CAT'S FAVOURITE DAY

MEALS

Breakfast:

Lunch:

Dinner:

Snacks:

NAP TIMES

Morning:

Noon:

Night:

GAMES

-
-
-

ECCENTRICITIES

What freaks out your fur buddy?

How do you know if your cat has been spooked?

From squeals and squeaks to caterwauling, how does your cat talk to you?

What is the strangest noise your cat makes and what do you think it means?

In what ways does your cat say 'I love you'?

_____

_____

_____

_____

_____

_____

_____

_____

_____

_____

_____

_____

A simple cardboard box has a wealth of play potential, but what other household things fascinate your feline?

●

●

●

●

●

What's the funniest thing they've done since joining the family?

What's the weirdest thing they've done since joining the family?

What is your cat's strangest habit?

Has your cat taken a dislike to anyone or anything; why do you think this is?

Do you watch TV together, and if so, which shows top your kitty's list?

From high-pitched wails to mellow purrs, cats have amazing vocal skills, but is yours a music lover, and if so, what's their favourite type of music/song?

Cats are the queens of clean, but is yours a water baby at heart? Any funny bathing stories?

If there's a space, there's a cat squeezed into it. Where does yours like to hide, and what is their oddest bolt hole?

Have they ever got stuck in a weird place?

What secret talents does your feline possess? Fence-walking, back flips, or the ability to hear a can of tuna being opened at more than ten paces away?

From half-eaten jam doughnuts to an old tennis ball, what's the weirdest gift your cat has given you and what are they trying to tell you?

What superpowers do you think they have?

What superpowers do they think they have?

And what can't they master, no matter how hard they try?

Describe the naughtiest thing your cat has ever done.

_____

_____

_____

_____

_____

_____

_____

_____

_____

_____

_____

Have they ever been in a fight with another cat?

From pen lids to paper clips, has your cat ever eaten something they shouldn't have?

How well behaved is your cat at the vet?

Are they a freaked-out feline or a take-it-easy top cat?

What are their views on cat carriers: a cosy safe haven or a cat prison?

What calms them down when the going gets tough?

Does your cat like to be brushed? A little hairdressing can go a long way to counteract hair balls.

Is there something naughty that they do that you regularly have to discourage?

Does your crazy cat have any quirky kitty antics?

What do they do that drives you up the wall?

PRACTICAL INFO

What's your cat's name?

What's their official date of birth?

What date did they join the family?

Do they have any known illnesses?

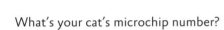

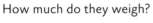

What's your cat's microchip number?

How much do they weigh?

What's your vet's name, address and contact details?

_____

_____

_____

_____

_____

_____

_____

_____

_____

_____

_____

_____

List any numbers and contact details in case of emergencies.

What vaccinations does your cat need? List details and dates.

-
-
-
-

How often do they need them?

When did your cat have its first flea and worm treatment?

How often do they need flea and worm treatments?

Does your cat have any allergies?

-
-
-

Give details of illnesses since joining the family.

-
-
-

List any regular medications, including times and dosages.

-
-
-
-
-

What is the condition of your cat's teeth?

How do you keep them clean?

List their grooming details (tools, dates and times).

-
-
-
-
-

Is anyone in your family allergic to cats?

What precautions will you take when family are visiting?

Will you spay or neuter your cat? Make a note of your arrangements for this.

_____

_____

_____

_____

_____

_____

_____

_____

_____

_____

_____

List your insurance details, reference numbers and any exclusions to the policy.

●

●

●

●

●

Do you have a cat sitter or a cattery you use? List the details.

zzz…

USE THIS PAGE TO WRITE INSTRUCTIONS FOR YOUR CAT SITTER

Breakfast:

Lunch:

Dinner:

Snacks:

How often does their litter tray need changing?

Curfew:

Does your cat use a cat flap or have a personal doorman?

Make a note of any other useful information.

-

-

-

Make a list of useful stores and websites for your cat's needs
and belongings.

-

-

-

-

-

-

NOTES

PUBLISHING DIRECTOR Sarah Lavelle

BUSINESS DEVELOPMENT DIRECTOR Melanie Gray

EDITOR Stacey Cleworth

WORDS Alison Davies

JUNIOR DESIGNER Alicia House

HEAD OF PRODUCTION Stephen Lang

PRODUCTION CONTROLLER Katie Jarvis

Published in 2021 by Quadrille,
an imprint of Hardie Grant Publishing

Quadrille
52–54 Southwark Street
London SE1 1UN
quadrille.com

ISBN 978 1 78713 542 0

Printed in China